Charles B. Gerard

Descendants of Ralph Chapman

Charles B. Gerard

Descendants of Ralph Chapman

ISBN/EAN: 9783337086534

Printed in Europe, USA, Canada, Australia, Japan

Cover: Foto ©ninafisch / pixelio.de

More available books at **www.hansebooks.com**

DESCENDANTS

OF

alph Chapman.

BY CHARLES B. GERARD.

NEWBURGH, N. Y.:
E. M. RUTTENBER & SON, PRINTERS.
1876

PREFACE.

VERY natural desire to know the names and origin of his ancestors, prompted the writer to make the necessary researches, and compile from local history and family records this genealogy. For the gratification of numerous members of the family who have shown an interest in the work, and of himself, as well as for the benefit of future generations, it has been put into its present form for preservation. Although not a complete genealogy of the family, it will be found very nearly so in respect to the descendants of the elder son of the emigrant ancestor.

Some liberty has been taken with a few of the records; names which were evidently improperly written in the diminutive, have been recorded in their proper forms, and the modern names of localities have in every case been substituted for the ancient ones.

The arrangement, the simplest and best one known to

the writer, will be no doubt readily understood by those into whose hands the book may fall, and by it the individual members of the family can easily trace their lineage to the common ancestor.

The writer requests that where a mistake or an omission is discovered, a correction of the mistake, or the data to supply the omission, may be forwarded to him, so that it may be entered in a copy kept for that purpose to serve to render a possible future edition more complete.

NEWBURGH. N. Y., July 4, 1876.

INTRODUCTORY.

THE name Chapman is one of a large class of English surnames that is derived from the names of trades or occupations. It is of Saxon origin, and the original word, *ceapman*, means a purchaser, a buyer or a merchant. It is one of the oldest of English surnames, and was adopted, according to local history, as early as the twelfth century.

In the United States there are several extensive families of the name of Chapman, descendants of the early settlers of that name in New England, Virginia, Maryland and Pennsylvania. A list of these, who were probably not in the remotest degree related, and who emigrated at different times and from widely separated localities, is given below:

It is recorded that John Chapman was admitted a resident of Boston in 1634. Ralph Chapman left England in April 1635. Henry Chapman left England for Virginia, in ship *Alice*, July 1635, aged 44. Richard Chapman left England in ship *Elizabeth*, Aug. 1, 1635, aged 18. Thomas Chapman left England in the *Globe* of

London, for Virginia, Aug. 7, 1635, aged 26. Robert Chapman* settled in Connecticut in 1635. John Chapman appears among a list of planters in New Haven in 1643. Edward Chapman had a land grant at Ipswich in 1644. Robert Chapman was one of the earliest settlers of New Hampshire. William Chapman appears in the records of New London, Conn., in 1657. Edward Chapman appears in the records of Windsor, Conn., in 1660.

Besides the above, the name occurs in the early records of Rhode Island, and in Pennsylvania one of the name of Chapman settled about Penn's time; his descendants are now very numerous in that state.

Ralph Chapman, second in the list of names given above, emigrated from the parish of St. Saviors, Southwark,† County Surrey, England, in April 1635, as appears by the following record from "The Register of "the names of all ye passengers who passed from ye Port "of London for an whole yeare ending at X mas 1635:

"XIII Apriles: In the *Elizabeth* de Lo:‡ Mr.§ prd.‖ theis "underwritten names brought cert.¶ from the ministers "of St. Saviors, Southwark, of their conformitie :*2
"Thomas Millet, æ 30.   Joseph Wheat, æ 17.
"Maria Millet, uxor, æ 29.   Henri Bull, æ 19.
"Thomas Millet, æ 2.   Ralph Chapman, æ 20."

Nothing is known of Ralph or his family prior to the

---

* A genealogy of his descendants has been published.
† One of the wards of London, termed the "Bridge Ward Without."
‡ Of London. § Master. ‖ Produce. ¶ Certificates.
*2 Conformity to the Established Church.

date of the foregoing record, and the little that is known
of his subsequent career or of his immediate descendants,
can be told in a very few words. He probably settled
in Duxbury on his arrival in Plymouth Colony, although
no mention is made of him in the records until 1640,
five years after his departure from London. In that
year he was a resident of Duxbury, and had some land
granted to him, as appears from the following record :

"At a Court of Assistants held at Plymouth aforesaid
"the first day of June, in the xvi yeare of the now raigne
"of our Souveraigne Lord Charles, by the Grace of
"God King of England, &c.

"Before William Bradford, Gent., Gov. Thomas
"Prence, John Alden, William Collyer, Timothy
"Hatherly, Capt. Miles Standish, John Jamey and
"John Browne, Gents, Assistants, &c.

"John Phillips, James Lindall, William Sherman, Ed-
"mond Weston, Samuel Tompkins, Arthur Harrison,
"and Ralph Chapman of Duxborrow are granted foure
"acres apeece of upland abutting upon the Stony Brooke
"in Duxborrow, by the milne, and to rang* North and
"South in length, and East and West in breadth."†

Two years after he was granted land as follows:

"At the General Court of our Souveraigne Lord
"Charles, by the Grace of God King of England, &c.,
"March 7, 1642, Ralph Chapman is granted a parcel of
"land lying at Namassacuset, to that he hath bought of
"Peter Collyer there."‡

* Range.   † Plymouth Records, Mass. Hist. Coll.
‡ Plymouth Records, Mass. Hist. Coll.

In 1645 he bought a ferry privilege at New Harbor Marshes of Robert Barker, and soon after petitioned the Court to excuse him, "as it would bring him to extreme poverty," which they did, except on special occasions, as bringing over the magistrates.*

Two or three unimportant records show that he became a resident of the town of Marshfield about the year 1650. He lived there until his death, which took place in the early part of the year 1671, as shown by the following Court record:

"Att the Court of his Majestie held att Plymouth, for "the jurisdiction of New Plymouth, the fifth day of "March, Anno Dom. 1671—

"Before Thomas Prence, Esquire, Gov. John Alden,
	"William Bradford, Josiah Winslow, Thomas Hin-
	"cley, and Nathaniel Bacon, Assistants, &c.

"In reference unto the estate of Ralph Chapman, de-"ceased, altho' the Court is not satisfyed in some respects "concerning his will, notwithstanding they have ordered "and doe request Edward Wanton of Scittuate to look "unto and take care of the said estate for the preserva-"tion and improvement thereof and of his land, and to "keep an account of his doeings about it untill the "Court shall see cause otherwise to order."

An abstract of the Will referred to reads:

"Ralph Chapman, Marshfield—To da.† Sarah and her "husband, Wm. Norcutt; to younger son Ralph; to "children Samuel, John and Mary. 28 Nov. 1670. "Witnessed by Peregrine White, Eph. Little, William

	* Winsor's History of Duxbury.			† Daughter.

" Ford, Sr., aged 67, Thomas Little, aged 50, Anna Little,
" aged 60, Eph Little, aged 22, testify that at the making
" of his will Ralph Chapman's hands were so swelled
" that he could not sign it. Inventory £46, 5s. 9d."

Isaac Chapman, the elder son of Ralph, settled at an
early age in or near Rochester, Mass., and probably
learned his trade of Colonel James Leonard, who had
early established a forge at that place. He married
Rebecca, Colonel Leonard's daughter, and about the
year 1689 removed to Barnstable, Mass; the exact date
is not known, but the following extract of a deed from
Henry Cobb of Barnstable, fixes the probable date of
the first appearance of the Chapman family on Cape Cod :

" To all people to whom these presents shall come :
" Henry Cobb of Barnstable, in the Colony of New
" Plymouth, in New England, planter, sendeth greeting,
" &c. Know ye that I, the said Henry Cobb, for a valu-
" able consideration in a certain parcel of upland to me
" in exchange given by and granted by Isaak Chapman
" of Barnstable aforesaid, blacksmith, the receipt whereof
" &c., by these presents do in exchange give, grant,
" bargain, &c., all that my parcel of upland containing
" six acres, more or less, and four hundred acres of
" marsh, be it more or less, lying and being near unto
" the hill commonly called Cobb's Hill, and is bounded
" southerly by the lands of John Davis, and northerly
" by the lands of Samuel Sarjant, partly by John Davis,
" and partly by a creek ; easterly partly by the highway
" that leads to Blackinson's Creek, and partly by a little
" creek that divides it from the marsh of Jonathan Cobb ;

" and northerly by the said Jonathan Cobb, according
": to the known and ascertained boundaries thereof, &c.
" In witness whereof, I the said Henry Cobb have here-
" unto set my hand and seal this twentieth day of De-
" cember, Anno Domini one thousand six hundred and
" eighty-nine."

He settled in the town of Yarmouth, in that part that
is now the town of Dennis, Mass., about the year 1696,*
and lived there until his death, which occurred in his
ninetieth year. The land that he owned there has been
in possession of, and the house that he built has ever
since been occupied by, his descendants.

Ralph Chapman the younger, son of the emigrant,
became a member of the Society of Friends, and early
settled in Scittuate, Mass., where he married. He removed from there about the year 1680, and settled in the
town of Newport, Rhode Island. The records of the
family were kept in the books of the Society until about
the year 1720, at which time, from some unknown cause,
the family ceased their connection with the Friends at
that place. From that time the history of the family
is very obscure, and it is only from one of the descendants of the younger Ralph that the family can be traced
to the present generation. This one, John Chapman, a
grandson of the younger Ralph, left Newport at an
early age and settled near Hanover, Mass., where, as the
record of his family shows, he died at the remarkable
age of one hundred and four years.

* Freeman's History of Cape Cod.

CHAPMAN.

RALPH CHAPMAN, born in Southwark, Surrey county, England, in the year 1615; died in Marshfield, Mass., in the year 1671; married, November 23, 1642, Lydia Wills, of Duxbury, Mass.

CHILDREN.

1	Mary[2]	b. Oct 31, 1643.	. . . .
2	Sarah[2]	" May 15, 1645.	. . . .
3	Isaac[2]	" Aug. 4, 1647,	d. Jan. 9, 1737.
4	Lydia[2]	" Nov. 26, 1649,	" Nov. 26, 1649.
5	Ralph[2]	" Feb. 20, 1651,	" July 29, 1653.
	. . . . . . [*]	. . . .	. . . .
6	Ralph[2]	 165-,	

I.

MARY CHAPMAN,[2] born in Duxbury, Mass., Oct. 31,

* Probably John and Samuel. See Appendix.

1643; married, May 14, 1666, William Troop of Barnstable, Mass.

CHILDREN.

7 Mary[3]   b. April 6, 1667.   ....
8 Thomas[3]   ....

2.

SARAH CHAPMAN,[2] born May 15, 1645, died -:
married William Norcutt of Marshfield, Mass, born ——,
died Sept. 18, 1693.

CHILDREN.

9 Ralph[3]   d. Dec. 2, 1715.
10 William[3]   ....
11 John[3]   ....
12 Thomas[3]
13 Isaac[3]
14 Ephraim[3]   ....
15 Ebenezer[3]
16 Lydia[3]
17 Anne[3]
18 Sarah[3]
19 Patience[3]
20 Experience[3] ....

3.

ISAAC CHAPMAN,[2] born in Marshfield, Mass., Aug. 4,
1647, died in Dennis, Mass., January 9, 1737; married,

Sept. 2, 1678, Rebecca Leonard, daughter of Col. James Leonard of Rochester, Mass., born 1657, died in Dennis, Mass., March 15, 1736.

CHILDREN.

21 Lydia[3]	b. Dec. 15, 1679,	d. Sept. 4, 1760.	
22 John[3]	" May 12, 1681.	. . . .	
23 Hannah[3]	" Dec. 26, 1682,	" July 6, 1689.	
24 James[3]	" Aug. 5, 1685.		
25 Abigail[3]	" July 11, 1687.		
26 Hannah[3]	" April 10, 1690.	. . . .	
27 Isaac[3]	" Dec. 29, 1692,	" Dec. 12, 1776.	
28 Ralph[3]	" Jan. 19, 1695,	" Feb. 8, 1779.	
29 Rebecca[3]	" June 10, 1697,	" June 24, 1777.	

6.

RALPH CHAPMAN,[2] of Newport, R. I., born in Marshfield, Mass., —— 165–, died ——; married first, Mary ——, born ——, died in Newport March 22, 1688; married second, Abigail ——, born ——, died ——; married third, Mary, daughter of Walter Clark, Esq., of Newport, born Jan. 11, 1661, died in Newport Aug. 10, 1711.

CHILDREN BY FIRST WIFE.

30 Ralph[3]	b. Jan. 7, 1679–80,	d. Feb. 7, 1728.	
31 John[3]	" Aug. 5, 1682.	. . . .	
32 Isaac[3]	" Dec. 29, 1684,	" Feb. 7, 1765.	
33 William[3]	" March 7, 1686–7,	" March 13, 1688.	

CHILDREN BY SECOND WIFE.

34 Abigail[3]	b. Sept. ..., 1691.	d. Oct. 10, 1713.

35 Lydia[3]   b. .... .., 1694.   d. .... .., 1708.

21.

LYDIA CHAPMAN,[3] born Dec. 15, 1679, died Sept. 4, 1760; married John Dillingham, born ——, died Sept. 11, 1746.

CHILDREN.

36 John[4]	b. March 23, 1702.	d. .... .., 1763.
37 Elisa[4]	" Aug. 2, 1703.	
38 Lydia[4]	" June 21, 1705.	
39 Hannah[4]	" Feb. 2, 1706-7.	
40 Rebecca[4]	" June 24, 1709.	....
41 Isaac[4]	" May 4, 1711.	
42 Abigail[4]	" June 2, 1713.	
43 Edward[4]	" May 17, 1715.	
44 Thankful[4]	" April 18, 1718.	....
45 Sarah[4]	" Feb. 10, 1719-20.	....

22.

JOHN CHAPMAN,[3] born May 12, 1681, probably settled in Taunton, Mass., where his father owned lands, and was probably the ancestor of the Chapman families of Taunton whose records are given in the Appendix.

24.

JAMES CHAPMAN,[3] of Rochester, Mass., born August 5, 1685, died ——; married Mehitable — .

Probably no issue. There was none as late as 1724.

25.

ABIGAIL CHAPMAN,[3] born July 11, 1687; died   ;
unmarried.

26.

HANNAH CHAPMAN,[3] born April 10, 1690; died ——;
married Ebenezer Holmes, of Rochester, Mass.

CHILDREN.

46 John[4]	b. Aug. 19, 1717.	. . . .
47 Barnabas[4]	" May 5, 1719.	. . . .
48 Ebenezer[4]	" Sept. 3, 1720.	
49 Seth[4]	" Dec. 22, 1721.	. . . .
50 Rebecca[4]	" March 8, 1723.	. . . .
51 Lydia[4]	" Feb. 22, 1724.	
52 Hannah[4]	" Dec. 17, 1727.	. . . .

27.

ISAAC CHAPMAN,[3] born Dec. 29, 1692; died in Dennis,
Mass., Dec. 12, 1776; married first, Elizabeth ——, born
1699; died in Dennis 1754; married second, Priscilla
——, born 1709–10; died in Dennis Sept. 24, 1764.

CHILDREN BY FIRST WIFE.

53 Isaac[4]	b. April 7, 1721,	d. about 1780.
54 Mary[4]	" June 6, 1723,	" July 8, 1778.
55 Rebecca[4]	" Nov. 14, 1726,	" Dec. 30, 1726.
56 Samuel[4]	" Nov. 14, 1727,	" Oct. 3, 1758.
57 Rebecca[4]	" June 25, 1730.	. . . .

58 Ruth[4]	b. April 13, 1733,	d. Sept. 30, 1801.
59 Micah[4]	" July 18, 1735,	" Oct. 29, 1792.

28.

RALPH CHAPMAN,[3] born January 19, 1695; died in Dennis, Mass., Feb. 8, 1779; married Elizabeth Wing of Sandwich, Mass, born 1699 1700; died in Dennis July 4, 1783.

CHILDREN.

60 John[4]	b. Feb. 22, 1728,	d. Nov. 9, 1815.
61 Elizabeth[4]	" Oct. 15, 1736.	. . . .
62 David[4]	" Nov. 15, 1739,	" April 13, 1830.

29.

REBECCA CHAPMAN,[3] born in Dennis, Mass., June 10, 1697; died in Southeast, Putnam county, N. Y, June 24, 1777. Married first, John Paddock, born in Dennis, Mass., 1694; died Sept. 30, 1732. Married second, Norris of Southeast, N. Y.

CHILDREN.

63 Ann[4]	b. Oct. 25, 1716,	d. June 30, 1717.
64 Mary[4]	" June .., 1720,	" Nov. 20, 1728.
65 Elizabeth[4]	" .... .., 1722,	" April 2, 1725.
66 Mary[4]	" March 27, 1732,	" April 6, 1732.

30.

RALPH CHAPMAN,[3] born in Scittuate, Mass., Jan. 7,

1679-80, died in Newport, R. I., Feb. 7, 1728; married first, Deliverance Slocum, born 1685, died in Newport Aug. 11, 1711; married second, Ann ——.

CHILDREN BY FIRST WIFE.

67 John⁴   b. Feb. ... 1707,   d. May 3, 1811.
Probably several other children.

CHILDREN BY SECOND WIFE.

68 Ann⁴   b. ... ..., 1721,   d. Jan. 31, 1722.
69 William⁴   " ... ..., 1726,   " Aug. 8, 1727.

35.

ISAAC CHAPMAN³, born in Newport, R. I., December 29, 1684, died in Newport Feb. 7, 1765; married Mary - --, born 1697; died Sept. 24, 1759, in Newport.

CHILDREN.

70 Isaac⁴   b. May 28, 1715.
71 James⁴   " July 4, 1717.   ....
72 Mary⁴   " 1720,   d. March 28, 1720.
73 John⁴   " June 20, 1724.

53.

ISAAC CHAPMAN,⁴ born in Dennis, Mass., April 7, 1721; settled about 1740 in Southeast, Putnam county, N. Y., where he died about the year 1780; married Mary Paddock, born in Dennis, Mass., June 3, 1724; died in Southeast, N. Y., Nov. 8, 1776.

CHILDREN.

74 Peter⁵   b. April 19, 1743,   d. Oct. 11, 1776.

75 Mary[5]	b. Jan. 4, 1745.	d..............
76 Isaac[5]	" June 27, 1747,	" May 12, 1761.
77 Noah[5]	" April 28, 1749.	....
78 Elizabeth[5]	" Nov. 15, 1752.	
79 Enoch[5]	" June 8, 1755.	....
80 Samuel[5]	" March 31, 1759.	....
81 Thomas[5]	" May 5, 1760,	" June 6, 1827.
82 Abigail[5]	" June 27, 1762,	" May 1, 1778.

54.

MARY CHAPMAN,[4] born in Dennis, Mass, June 6, 1723; died in Southeast, N. Y., July 8, 1778; married Thomas Paddock, born in Dennis, Mass., 1723, died in Southeast, N. Y., January 17, 1799. No issue.

56.

SAMUEL CHAPMAN,[4] born in Dennis, Mass., Nov. 14, 1727; died in Dennis Oct. 3, 1758, unmarried.

57.

REBECCA CHAPMAN,[4] born in Dennis, Mass., June 25, 1730, died ——; married —— Howes of——.

58.

RUTH CHAPMAN,[4] born in Dennis, Mass., April 13, 1733, died in Southeast, N. Y., Sept. 30, 1801; married Reuben Doane of Southeast, N. Y.

CHILDREN.

83 Reuben[5] ....

84 Joshua[5] . . . .
85 Sarah[5] . . . .
And others, names unknown.

59.

MICAH CHAPMAN,[4] born in Dennis, Mass, July 18, 1735, died in Dennis Oct. 29, 1792; married Elizabeth Howes, born 1738, died in Dennis Aug. 26, 1820.

CHILDREN.

86 Elizabeth[5]	b. Jan. 19, 1761,	d. July 3, 1826.
87 Samuel[5]	" May 23, 1764,	" March 30, 1794.
88 Howes[5]	" June 16, 1768,	" . . . . . ., 1787.
89 Isaac[5]	" April 27, 1770,	" Aug. 27, 1834.
90 Mary[5]	" July 1, 1775,	" March 4, 1801.

60.

JOHN CHAPMAN,[4] born in Dennis, Mass., Feb. 22, 1728, died in Dennis Nov. 9, 1815; married Hannah Lincoln, born 1730, died —

CHILDREN.

91 Hannah[5]	. . . .	. . . .
92 Lydia[5]	b. Feb. 9, 1751,	d. March 29, 1758.
93 Deborah[5]	" Jan. 16, 1755,	. . . .
94 Lydia[5]	" Aug. 31, 1758,	" June 20, 1835.
95 John[5] ,	" May 2, 1761,	" Dec. 28, 1820.
96 Rebecca[5]	" Jan. 20, 1766,	" May 30, 1862.

61.

ELIZABETH CHAPMAN,[4] born in Dennis, Mass., Oct. 15,
1736, died ——; married Stephen Homer.

CHILDREN.

97 Chapman[5]   ....
98 Joshua[5]   ....
99 Stephen[5]   ....
100 Joseph[5]   ....
101 William[5]   ....
102 Zenas[5]   ....
103 David[5]   ....
104 Benjamin[5]   ....
105 Elizabeth[5]   ....
106 Bethia[5]   ....
107 Name unknown.   ....
108 "   "   ....
109 "   "   ....
110 "   "   ....

62.

DAVID CHAPMAN,[4] born in Dennis, Mass., Nov. 15,
1739; died in Dennis April 13, 1830; married first,
Thankful Nye, born 1738-9; died Sept. 16, 1763; married second, Elizabeth Hinckley, born 1738-9; died
Sept. 8, 1814.

CHILDREN.

111 Thankful[5] b. June .., 1769,   d. March 26, 1857.

112 Benjamin H.[5] b. .... .., 1773,   d. Aug. 29, 1797.
113 David[5]   " .... .., 1776,   " Nov. 25, 1799.

67.

JOHN CHAPMAN,[4] born Feb. —, 1707, in Newport, R. I. He settled in Hanover, Mass., at an early age, and died there May 3, 1811. "He retained to a remarkable "degree his health and vigor to the last. About two "years to his death he rode on horseback a distance of "nine miles to visit his great grand-daughter, that he "might hold on his knees her two children, his descend-"ants in the fifth generation."* He married, in June 1730, Sarah Booth of Pembroke, Mass.

CHILDREN.

[FROM RECORDS OF FRIENDS SOCIETY, PEMBROKE.]

114 Ralph[5]
115 Abigail[5]   b. .... .., 1733-4, d. Dec. 1, 1821.
116 Deliverance[5]" June 4, 1736,   " .... .., 1766.
117 Sarah[5]   " Sept. 5, 1738.   ....
118 John[5]   " June 6, 1741,   " May 20, 1839.
119 Mary[5]   " Jan. 2, 1743.   ....
120 William[5]   " Nov. 6, 1745.   ....
121 Abraham[5]

70, 71 or 73.

The last record of the Chapman family in the books of the Friends Society at Newport, R. I., is that of

---

* From Winsor's History of Duxbury, Mass.

Isaac's (32) children.   As the early records of the town
of Newport were almost entirely destroyed during the
Revolutionary war, it is impossible to get the names of
the family in the fourth generation.   The few members
of the Chapman family now living in Newport have a
tradition that they are descendants of Ralph Chapman.
That they are descendants of Isaac (70), James (71), or
John (73), is conjectural.

122. Name unknown.   Son of 70, 71 or 73.

74.

PETER CHAPMAN,[5] born April 19, 1743; died in Southeast, Putnam county, N. Y., October 11, 1776; married
Mary Elwell of Southeast, N. Y.

CHILDREN.

123 Ruth[6]	b. Feb. 25, 1771.	. . . .
124 Isaac[6]	" May 8, 1773,	d. Feb. 10, 1856.
125 Anna[6]	" April 23, 1775.	

75.

MARY CHAPMAN,[5] born in Southeast, N. Y., Jan. 4,
1745, married ——— Crane. This family lived in Connecticut, and in the township adjoining the town of
Southeast, Putnam county, N. Y.*

CHILDREN.

126 . . . .

* The record of this family was promised me. The number of children
being known, the spaces were left for the names, but up to the time of publi-
cation have been unable to obtain them.—*C. B. G.*

127 ....'..   ....
128 ....
129 ....
130 ....
131 ....
132 ....
133 ....
134 ....
135 ....'' ....

77.

NOAH CHAPMAN,[5] born in Southeast, N. Y., April 28, 1749. Judging from the tone of a letter written by his mother to his Uncle Micah, dated June 1777, it is very probable that he died at sea in that year. He was unmarried in 1777.

78.

ELIZABETH CHAPMAN,[5] born Nov. 15, 1752; married William Young of Southeast, N. Y. They had a number of children whose names are unknown.

79.

ENOCH CHAPMAN,[5] born in Southeast, N. Y., June 8, 1755; died about ——, in Friendship, Alleghany Co., N. Y. He was for many years a resident of Sherburne, N. Y. He married Chloe Gage, daughter of Ebenezer Gage

of Cape Cod, born ———; died Nov. 30, 1840, in Friendship, N. Y.

CHILDREN.

136 Enoch[6]	. . . .	
136 Enoch[6]	. . . .	. . . .
137 Peter G.[6]	b. July 17, 1785,	d. Dec. 26, 1841.
138 Isaac[6]	" March 14, 1788,	" July 30, 1853.
139 Mary P.[6]	" March 28, 1790,	" Dec. 25, 1868.
140 Chloe[6]	" May 20, 1792,	" June 12, 1828.
141 Sarah[6]	. . . .	. . . .

80.

SAMUEL CHAPMAN,[5] born in Southeast, N. Y., March
31, 1759; died unmarried.

81.

THOMAS CHAPMAN,[5] born in Southeast, Putnam Co.,
N. Y., May 5, 1760; died in Southeast June 6, 1827;
married, January 30, 1782, Deborah Close, daughter of
Nathaniel Close of North Salem, Westchester Co., N.Y.
She was born August 20, 1765, and died in Michigan
City, Ind., January 31, 1854.

CHILDREN.

142	b. Nov. 21, 1783,	d. Dec. 5, 1783.
143 Sarah[6]	" Jan. 8, 1785,	" Aug. 9, 1870.
144 Mary[6]	" March 28, 1787.	. . . .
145 Paddock[6]	" Jan. 17, 1790,	" April 2, 1865.
146 Peter	" Aug. 31, 1792,	" January 30, 1847.

147 Cyrene[6]	b. June 18, 1795,	d. Oct. 17, 1823.
148 Samuel[6]	" Dec. 6, 1797.	....
149 Isaac[6]	" May 23, 1800,	" August —, 1838.
150 Marilda[6]	" Oct. 8, 1802.	" Feb. 1, 1869.
151 James[6]	" Aug. 11, 1805,	" Feb. 26, 1807.
152 Maria[5]	" Dec. 27, 1808,	" March 16, 1868.

86.

ELIZABETH CHAPMAN,[5] born in Dennis, Mass., Jan. 19, 1761 ; died July 3, 1826. Married Benjamin Lathrop. No issue.

87.

SAMUEL CHAPMAN,[5] born in Dennis, Mass., May 23, 1764; died in the West Indies, March 30, 1794; married Mary Hall. No issue.

89.

ISAAC CHAPMAN,[5] born in Dennis, Mass., April 27, 1770; died in same town August 27, 1834; married, January 17, 1799, Hannah Bassett of Barnstable, Mass.

CHILDREN.

153 Samuel[6]	b. July 9, 1800,	d. Sept. 6, 1824.
154 ElizabethH.[6]"	April 23, 1802.	
155 Mary B.[6]	" June 11, 1804.	....
156 Micah[6]	" July 26, 1806,	" Sept. 23, 1824.
157 Isaac[6]	" Oct. 20, 1809,	" March 28, 1862.
158 Howes[6]	" Nov. 1, 1812.	....

159 Elisha B.[6]   b. Jan. 27, 1815,   d. Aug. 29, 1835.
160 Hannah B.[6]   " April 28, 1817.   . . . .
161 Noah[6]   " Oct. 31, 1821,   " Oct. 9, 1824.

90.

MARY CHAPMAN,[5] born July 1, 1775; died in Dennis,
Mass, March 4, 1801. Unmarried.

91.

HANNAH CHAPMAN,[5] born in Dennis, Mass., 1749;
married John Eldridge of — -, born Feb. 14. 1743: died
Jan. 6, 1797.

CHILDREN.

162 Abigail[6]   b. Jan. 26, 1773.   . . . .
163 Ruth[6]   " Nov. 1, 1775,   d. Oct. 12, 1848.
164 Hannah[6]   " Dec. 3, 1777,   " Jan. 15, 1852.
165 Mary[6]   " March 3, 1780.   . . . .
166 Rebecca[6]   " May 9, 1782,   " Oct. 26, 1870.
167 Deborah[6]   " Aug. 9, 1784,   " June 8, 1870.
168 Lydia[6]   " Feb. 20, 1787,   " July 9, 1835.
169 John[6]   " Oct. 16, 1789,   " Sept. 22, 1871.
170 Joshua[6]   " July 2, 1792,   " Dec. 20, 1861.
171 Gorham[6]   " Nov. 2, 1794.   . . . .
172 Samuel[6]   " Feb. 2, 1797.

93.

DEBORAH CHAPMAN,[5] born in Dennis, Mass., Jan. 16,
1755; died in Waterville, Maine; married, Dec. 7, 1776.

Solomon Hallett of Yarmouth, Mass., born November
23, 1754; died —— in Waterville, Maine.

CHILDREN.

173 Ruth[6]   b. May 6, 1780.   ....
174 Isaiah[6] " Nov. 9, 1783.   ....

94.

LYDIA CHAPMAN,[5] born in Dennis, Mass,, Aug. 31,
1758; died June 20, 1835; married, Nov. 1784, Isaiah
Howes, born July 1, 1757; died May 18, 1835.

CHILDREN.

175 Achsah[6] b. Dec. 27, 1785, d. Sept. 10, 1872.
176 Isaiah[6] " July 10, 1788,   " Sept. ... 1873.
177 Sophia[6] " Aug. 3, 1791,   " .... 1868.
178 Lydia[6]   " April 13, 1794, " Sept. 29, 1867.
179 Alvan[6]   " Nov. 27, 1799,   " June 15, 1871.

95.

JOHN CHAPMAN,[5] born in Dennis, Mass., May 2, 1761,
died Dec. 28, 1820; married Hannah Paine, born ——,
died in Dennis Nov. 11, 1835.

CHILDREN.

180 Sarah[6]   b. April 16, 1783, d. Sept. 7, 1864.
181 Reuben[6]   " Jan. ..., 1784,   " Aug. ..., 1816.
182 James[6]   " July 19, 1787,   " .... 1816.
183 Ruth[6]   " Jan. 11, 1790,   " July 3, 1839.
184 Nathan[6]   " Oct. 11, 1798.   ....
185 Abraham[6] " June 27, 1803.   ....
186 John[6]   " May 30, 1805,   " March 29, 1872.

96.

REBECCA CHAPMAN,[5] born in Dennis, Mass., Jan. 20, 1766, died in Orleans, Mass., May 30, 1862; married Joseph Seabury, born in Brewster, Mass., Sept. 11, 1762, died in Orleans March 27, 1800.

CHILDREN.

187	Deborah[6]	b. Dec. 7, 1782,	d. July 1, 1860.
188	Benjamin[6]	" May 20, 1784,	" Sept. .., 1853.
189	Joseph[6]	" March 4, 1786,	" Sept. 29, 1809.
190	Isaac[6]	" May 8, 1788,	" Aug. 6, 1858.
191	John[6]	" Feb. 4, 1790,	" Aug. 5, 1848.
192	Nathan[6]	" June 18, 1791,	" Nov. 2, 1813.
193	Temperance[6]	" Jan. 20, 1793.	....
194	George[6]	" Jan. 4, 1795.	....
195	Sarah[6]	" Dec. 24, 1796,	" Aug. .., 1834.
196	Chapman[6]	" March 4, 1799,	" Jan. 8, 1861.

111.

THANKFUL CHAPMAN,[5] born June 1769, died March 26, 1857; married Stephen Homer, born 1764, died April 6, 1840.

CHILDREN.

197	Joshua[6]	b. Aug. 26, 1794.	....
198	Stephen[6]	....	d. May 17, 1875.
199	David C.[6]	....	....
200	Elizabeth H[6]	" ... .., 1798,	" Oct. 8, 1819.
201	Joseph[6]	" ... .., 1803,	" Aug. 1, 1828.
202	Thankful[6]	" ... .., 1810,	" April 27, 1828.

203 Benjamin H.[6] b............... d...............
204 Zenas[6]   " ...., 1814,   " June 10, 1849.

112.

BENJAMIN H. CHAPMAN,[5] born in Dennis. Mass., ——-,
1773, died in Santa Cruz, W. I., Aug. 29, 1797, unmarried.

113.

DAVID CHAPMAN,[5] born in Dennis, Mass., 1776, died
in Surinam, Dutch Guiana, Nov. 25, 1799, unmarried.

114.

RALPH CHAPMAN[5] of Hanover, Mass., born about 1732 ;
married Prudence Coleman.

CHILD.

205. Prudence[6] .... d. March .., 1829.

115.

ABIGAIL CHAPMAN,[5] born 1733-4, died Dec. 1, 1821 ;
married Ignatius Sherman of Marshfield, Mass.

116.

DELIVERANCE CHAPMAN,[5] born June 4. 1736, died
1766; married Wing Rogers of Marshfield, Mass.

117.

SARAH CHAPMAN,[5] born Sept. 5, 1738; married John
Rogers of Marshfield, Mass.

118.

JOHN CHAPMAN,[5] born in Hanover, Mass., June 6,*
1741, died in Hanover May 20, 1839; married first, Ruth
Torry, May 13, 1766; married second, Abigail Bates,
March 22, 1786; married third, Bethia Gardner, Dec.
14, 1790; she was born 1758, died Dec. 1841.

CHILDREN BY FIRST WIFE.

206 John[6]		Died young.
207 Joseph[6]		" "
208 Ruth[6]	. . . .	" "
209 Sarah[6]	. . . .	
210 Mary[6]	. . . .	. . . .
211 Name unknown.	. . . .	. . . .

CHILDREN BY SECOND WIFE.

212. Abigail   . . . .

CHILDREN BY THIRD WIFE.

213 John[6]	b. . . . . . ., 1791,	d. . . . . . ., 1809.	
214 Ruth[6]	. . . .	. . . .	
215 Joseph[6]	. . . .		
216 Daniel[6]	" Jan. 27, 1800.		
217 Edwin[6]	" April . ., 1802.	. . . .	
218 Kilborn[6]	" May 6, 1805,	" Nov. 16, 1865.	

119.

MARY CHAPMAN,[5] born Jan. 2, 1743; married Joseph
Rogers of Marshfield, Mass.—*Friends Society Records,
Pembroke, Mass.*

* Family record says June 17, —.

122.

—— CHAPMAN,[5] of Newport, R. I.

CHILDREN.

219 Ralph[6] ....
220 Brenton[6] ....
221 —— ....
222 —— ....

123.

RUTH CHAPMAN,[6] born in Southeast, N. Y., February 25, 1771; married Samuel Waring. Family resided in Cicero, N. Y.

CHILDREN.

223 Ada[7] ....
224 Lucinda[7] ....
225 Anna[7] ....
226 Isaac[7] ....

124.

ISAAC CHAPMAN,[6] born in Southeast, N. Y., May 8th, 1773; settled about the year 1800 in Sherburne, N. Y.; about 1852 removed to Granby, N. Y., where he died Feb. 10, 1856; married, Dec. 7, 1794, Sally Wooster, born in Southeast, N.Y., Oct. 21, 1799, died in Granby, N.Y., Jan. 2, 1862.

CHILDREN.

227 Harriet A.[7] b. Sept. 15, 1795. ....
228 Anna M.[7] " March 27, 1797, d. April 26, 1863.

229 Polly M.[7]   b, Feb. 10, 1799,   d. June 30, 1870.
230 Peter[7]   " Feb. 13, 1802,   " May 10, 1874.
231 Charles W.[7] " Dec. 17, 1803,   " Dec. 27, 1870.
232 William W.[7] " May 8, 1807.   ....
233 Lucius L.[7]   " Oct. 30, 1809.
234 Hannah[7]   " Aug. 30, 1811.
235 Emma Jane[7]   " July 18, 1817.
236 Laura L.[7]   " Oct. 8, 1819.   ....
237 Russel O.[7]   " Sept. 3, 1821,   " Sept. 24, 1870.

125.

ANNA CHAPMAN,[6] born in Southeast, N. Y., April 23, 1775; married Nathan Allen. This family lived in Syracuse, N. Y.

CHILDREN.

238 Elnathan[7]   b. Nov. 26, 1800.   ....
239 Polly M.[7]   ....
240 Harriet[7]   ....
241 Peter C.[7]   ....
242 Gould[7]   ....
243 Alfred[7]   ....

136.

ENOCH CHAPMAN,[6] born about 1783, settled in Erie county, Pa.; married Thankful Morehouse, born ———, died in Northeast, Erie county, Pa., Nov. —, 1845.

CHILDREN.

244 Sevillian[7]   ....

245 Lorenzo[7]   b. May 18, 1810.   . . . .
246 Deville[7]   . . . .
247 Minerva[7]   " Sept. 10, 1819,   d. June 2, 1848.
248. Delinda[7]   . . . .   " about 1867.

137.

PETER G. CHAPMAN,[6] born July 17, 1785, died in
Friendship, N. Y., Dec. 26, 1841 ; married Sarah Wilbur,
born Sept. 26, 1788, died July 12, 1869, in Wayne, Steu-
ben county, N. Y. Friendship, N. Y., family.

CHILDREN.

249 Livonia A.[7] b. June 5, 1810,   d. April 17, 1845.
250 Leander F.[7] " Sept. 26, 1812.   . . . .
251 Emily C.[7]   " Aug. 11, 1817,   " in infancy.
252 Margetta C.[7] " Nov. 13, 1818.   . . . .
253 J. Addison[7] " Sept. 4, 1821.   . . . . : . . .
254 Laura K.[7]   " April 1, 1826.   . . . .

138.

ISAAC CHAPMAN,[6] born in Pittstown, Rensselaer Co.,
N. Y., March 14, 1788, died in West Troy, N. Y., July
30, 1853. He was for many years superintendent of the
Watervliet Arsenal. He married Huldah Perkins of
Columbus, N. Y., born in Providence, R. I., June 4, 1789.
West Troy, N. Y., family.

CHILD.

250 Calista C.[7] b. . . . ., 1812,   d. Feb. 15, 1816.

139.

MARY P. CHAPMAN,[6] born March 28, 1790, died in Edinborough, Pa., Dec. 25, 1868; married, Nov. 16, 1808, Seymour Austin of Sherburne, N. Y., born Oct. 20, 1784, died July 16, 1854, in Edinborough, Pa.

CHILDREN.

256 Alzina[7]	b. Jan. 13, 1810,	d. .... .., 1812.
257 Nathaniel C.[7]	" Sept. 26, 1811.	....
258 VallorousG.[7]	" Oct. 30, 1814.	....
259 Susannah A.[7]	" Oct. 7, 1816.	....
260 Mary A.[7]	" April 22, 1819.	....
261 Hiram G.[7]	" Sept. 4, 1826.	....
262 Edwin C.[7]	" Dec. 11, 1828.	....

140.

CHLOE CHAPMAN,[6] born May 20, 1792, died June 12, 1828; married, Dec. 30, 1813, Nathan Herrick, born May 19, 1793, died at Bluff Point, Yates county, N. Y., Aug. 29, 1865. Family lived at Bluff Point.

CHILDREN.

263 Alzina M.[7]	b. July 3, 1815,	d. March 14, 1845.
264 Cyrus E.[7]	" Oct. 5, 1820,	" Nov. 17, 1872.
265 Sarah F.[7]	" Sept. 25, 1823,	" April 2, 1844.
266 Juliett[7]	" Jan. 14, 1825.	....

141.

SARAH CHAPMAN,[6] born —— 1794, died in town of Northeast, Erie county, Pa.; married ——— Shepherd. No issue.

143.

SARAH CHAPMAN,[6] born in Southeast, N. Y., January 8, 1785, died in Ashtabula, Ohio, Aug. 9, 1870; married, Nov. 6, 1804, Zenus Crosby, born in Southeast, N. Y., Dec. 12, 1783, died in Ashtabula, Ohio, July 30, 1868.

CHILDREN.

267 Orrin H.[7]   b. Feb. 24, 1806.   ....
268 Morgan B.[7]   " Dec. 17, 1808.
269 Thomas C.[7]   " May 12, 1811.   ....
270 Lewis M.[7]   " Feb. 2, 1814.   ....
271 Marilda[7]   " May 7, 1816,   d. May ..., 1852.
272 Calista[7]   " May 13, 1819.   ....
273 Peter E.[7]   " April 15, 1822, " ... ..., 1854.
274 Mary C.[7]   " Aug. 15, 1825,   " May 28, 1859.

144.

MARY CHAPMAN,[6] born in Southeast, N. Y., March 28, 1787; married, July 2, 1805, Eli Snow, born March 8, 1784, died Dec. 29, 1843. Family lived in N. Y. city.

CHILDREN.

275 Hart[7]   b. Aug. 18, 1806.   ....
276 Orville[7]   " July 28, 1809.   d. Feb. 4, 1829.
277 William[7]   " Sept. 3, 1811,   " Jan. 12, 1817.
278 Emeline[7]   " March 18, 1814, " Jan. 7, 1832.
279 Charlotte[7]   " Aug. 18, 1816,   " June 30, 1843.
280 Joshua[7]   " July 22, 1819,   " Sept. 18, 1841.
281 Isaac C.[7]   " July 24, 1823.   ....
282 Catharine M.[7] " March 25, 1827, " July 23, 1845.

282ª William T.[7] b. March 8, 1829.   . . . .
282ᵇ Eli[7]   " May 28, 1831,   d. Dec. 23, 1865.

145.

PADDOCK CHAPMAN,[6] born in Southeast, Putnam Co., N. Y., Jan. 17, 1790, settled about 1810 in Newburgh, Orange Co., N.Y., where he died April 2, 1865; married, May 4, 1820, Mary Hoffman, daughter of Joseph Hoffman, born in Newburgh, N. Y., Oct. 26, 1800, died Nov. 16, 1866. Newburgh, N. Y., family.

CHILDREN.

283 Mary E.[7]   b. March 16, 1821.   . . . .
284 JosephH.H[7] " March 12, 1823.   . . . .
285 CatharineM[7] " Dec. 1, 1824.   . . . .
286 Susan A.[7]   " Feb. 2, 1827.   . . . .
287 Deborah A.[7] " March 9, 1829.
288 Thomas P.[7] " June 1, 1831.
289 Isaac C.[7]   " July 31, 1833.
290 Charles F.[7]   " Aug. 5, 1835.   . . . .
291 James L.[7]   " Oct. 5, 1837,   d. January 4, 1840.
292 William G.[7] " Nov. 16, 1839.   . . . .
293 Caroline G.[7] " Dec. 21, 1842.   . . . .
294 Louisa[7]   " Jan. 23, 1845.   . . . .

146.

PETER CHAPMAN,[6] born in Southeast, N. Y., Aug. 31, 1792, died in Southeast Jan. 30, 1847; married, Nov. 17, 1813, Mary ———. No issue.

147.

CYRENE CHAPMAN,[6] born in Southeast, N. Y., June 18, 1795, died in Mobile, Alabama, Oct. 17, 1823; married, March 1815, Malcus R. Howes, born   , died in Mobile, Ala., 1832.

CHILDREN.

295 Cornelia A.[7] b. July 1, 1816.
296 James[7]   " .... ..1818.
297 William A.[7] " .... ..1820.

148.

SAMUEL CHAPMAN,[6] born in Southeast, N. Y., Dec. 6, 1797, died in Monticello, N. Y., unmarried.

149.

ISAAC CHAPMAN,[6] born in Southeast, N. Y., May 23, 1800, died Aug. 1838 in La Porte county, Indiana; married, Nov. 8, 1831, Hannah A. Howell, born in Albany, N. Y., Nov. 4, 1806.

CHILDREN.

298 William E.[7] b. Sept. 22, 1832.   ....
299 Alonzo R.[7] " April 14, 1834.   ....

150.

MATILDA CHAPMAN,[6] born in Southeast, N. Y., Oct. 8, 1802, died in Michigan City, Indiana, Feb. 1, 1869; married, April 12, 1832, Herman Lawson of Newburgh, N. Y., born ——, died in La Porte, Ind., 1863. No issue.

152.

MARIA CHAPMAN,[6] born in Southeast, N. Y., Dec. 27, 1808, died in Davenport, Iowa, March 16, 1868; married, May 16, 1831, Oscar A. Barker of Davenport, Iowa, born in Beekmantown, N. Y., 1806.

CHILD.

300 Samuel A.[7] b. March 3, 1832, d. July 1, 1860.

153.

SAMUEL CHAPMAN,[6] born July 9, 1800, died in Dennis Sept. 6, 1824, unmarried.

154.

ELIZABETH H. CHAPMAN,[6] born April 23, 1802, living in Dennis, Mass., (1875) unmarried.

155.

MARY B. CHAPMAN,[6] born in Dennis, Mass., June 11, 1804; married, Sept. 21, 1826, Stephen Homer, born ——, died in Dennis, Mass., May 17, 1875. Family reside in Dennis.

CHILDREN.

301 Joseph[7]	b. April 23, 1829,	d. Sept. 21, 1855.
302 Thankful[7]	" June 27, 1830.	. . . .
303 Margaret[7]	" Dec. 16, 1831.	. . . .
304 Catharine[7]	" Feb. 8, 1835,	" Sept. 5, 1869.
305 Elisha[7]	" Sept. 4, 1836.	. . . .

306 Minnie[7]   b. July 23, 1838,   d. Sept. 20, 1839.
307 Stephen[7]   " Jan. 27, 1840,   " Sept. 27, 1859.
308 Minnie[7]   " Oct. 25, 1848.   ....

157.

ISAAC CHAPMAN,[6] born in Dennis, Mass., Oct. 20, 1809, died March 28, 1862; married, June 5, 1834, Sophronia Howes, born in Brewster, Mass., Dec. 28, 1809. Family reside in Dennis, Mass.

CHILDREN.

309 Lois H.[7]   b. April 30, 1835.   ....
310 Samuel[7]   " March 6, 1837.   ....
311 Isaac H.[7]   " Dec. 4, 1838.   d. Jan. 27, 1845.
312 SophroniaH[7]   June 9, 1841,   " Jan. 19, 1845.
313 SophroniaH[7]   March 29, 1847.   ....

158.

HOWES CHAPMAN,[6] born in Dennis, Mass., Nov. 1, 1812; married, Nov. 2, 1838, Minerva Bassett, born in Barnstable, Mass., February 6, 1813, died in Dennis, Mass., Dec. 14, 1873. Family reside in Dennis, Mass.

CHILDREN.

314 Ruth B.[7]   b. Nov. 9, 1839,   d. Oct. 19, 1840.
315 John B.[7]   " July 3, 1841,   " Sept. 9, 1842.
316 Minerva H.[7]   " July 23, 1843.   ....
317 Nelson[7]   " May 20, 1845,   " March 11, 1846.
318 Nelson S.[7]   " April 25, 1847.   ....

160.

HANNAH B. CHAPMAN,[6] born in Dennis, Mass., April 28, 1817; married, Nov. 1836, Henry Bassett.

CHILDREN.

319	Elisha[7]	b. March 3, 1838.	....
320	Samuel[7]	" Oct. 20. 1839.	....
321	Henry[7]	" March 16, 1844.	....
322	Isaac[7]	" March 15, 1850.	
323	Hannah[7]	" Nov. 15, 1859.	....

180.

SARAH CHAPMAN,[6] born in Dennis, Mass., April 16, 1783, died Sept. 7, 1864; married, Dec. 23, 1814, Ichabod Seabury, born May 2, 1788, died Feb. 12, 1868.

CHILDREN.

324	David[7]	b. Jan. 28, 1816.	....
325	ElizabethA.[7]	" Dec. 19, 1820.	....
326	Rhoda[7]	" Jan. 2, 1822,	d. Oct. 6, 1873.
327	Joseph[7]	" March 2, 1825,	" June 12, 1853.
328	Reuben C.[7]	" Dec. 15, 1830.	....
329	John[7]	" Oct. 7, 1833.	....

181.

REUBEN CHAPMAN,[6] born in Dennis, Mass, Jan. 1784, died at sea Aug. 1816; married first, April 8, 1806, Mary Abbott, born in Tolland, Conn., March 29, 1784, died Nov. 30, 1807; married second, April 1810, Susan Paine of Eastham, Mass., born Oct. 26, 1789, died Aug. 18, 1856.

CHILD BY FIRST WIFE.

330 Reuben A.[7] b. Aug. 6, 1807. . . . .

CHILDREN BY SECOND WIFE.

331 Calvin[7]   b. Oct. 22, 1810,   d. Dec. 11, 1839.
332 Joseph[7]   " Dec. 10, 1812,   " May .., 1817.
333 Eben P.[7]   " July 6, 1815.   . . . .

182.

JAMES CHAPMAN,[6] born in Dennis, Mass., July 19, 1787, died at sea —— 1816; married, 1809, Mary Sears, born Feb. 6, 1790, died Jan. 5, 1830.

CHILDREN.

334 James[7]   b. March 7, 1810,   d. Oct. 10, 1856.
335 Henry[7]   " Oct. 22, 1811.   . . . .
336 Pamelia[7]   " Sept. 20, 1813.   . . . .
337 Mary[7]   " July 10, 1815,   " July 10, 1854.

183.

RUTH CHAPMAN,[6] born in Dennis, Mass., Jan. 11, 1790, died July 3, 1839; married. Nov. 29, 1806, Ebenezer Nickerson, born Sept. 24, 1783, died April 2, 1858.

CHILDREN.

338 Hannah C.[7] b. Nov. 11, 1807.   . . . .
339 Ruth[7]   " May 30, 1810.   . . . .
340 Nathan[7]   " Feb. 1, 1814.   d. August 2, 1842.
341, Mary A.[7]   " July 28, 1816.   . . . .
342 Sarah S.[7]   " Jan. 14, 1818,   " Feb. 20, 1865.
343 Perlina[7]   " Oct. 19, 1821.   . . . .

344 Loisa E.[7]   b. July 6, 1824,   d. Sept. 22, 1873.
345 Ebenezer[7]   " Feb. 18, 1827.   ....
346 Eunice C.[7]   " Aug. 18, 1829.

184.

NATHAN CHAPMAN,[6] born in Dennis, Mass., Oct. 11, 1798; married, 1820, Eliza Hopkins, born in Brewster, Mass., July 26, 1798. Living in 1875 in East Dennis, Mass.

CHILDREN.

347 Nathan[7]   b. July 11, 1821.   ....
348 David S.[7]   " Dec. 30, 1822.   ....
349 Eliza A.[7]   " March 15, 1824.
350 Benjamin F[7] " Jan. 21, 1826.   ....
351 Edmund H[7]   " Oct. 19, 1827.   d. April 1, 1849.
352 Mary F.[7]   " May 1, 1829.   ....
353 Harriet N.[7] " Jan. 9, 1832.   ....
354 George B.[7]   " Jan. 4, 1834.   " Jan. 10, 1871.
355 Horatio[7]   " Jan. 30, 1837.   ....
356 Charles C.[7] " April 29, 1842.

185.

ABRAHAM CHAPMAN,[6] born in Dennis, Mass, June 27, 1803; married first, Feb. 8, 1827, Eunice Howland, born May 12, 1805, died Sept. 20, 1828; married second, Elizabeth C. Gray, born July 4, 1814, died March 20, 1844; married third, April 2, 1845, Rebecca Kelly, born Sept. 15, 1817. Family live in E. Dennis, Mass.

CHILD BY FIRST WIFE.

357 Abraham[7]   b. March 9, 1828. ....

CHILDREN BY SECOND WIFE.

358 Eunice H.[7] b. June 16, 1836.
359 Henry R.[7] " Dec. 2, 1838.
360 Olive C.[7]   " March 2, 1841. ....

CHILDREN BY THIRD WIFE.

361 Elizabeth G[7] b. April 18, 1846. ....
362 Cecelia M.[7] " Sept. 22, 1848.
363 Carrie R.K.[7] " June 4, 1850.

186.

JOHN CHAPMAN,[6] born in Dennis, Mass, May 30, 1805,
died in Dennis Feb. 29, 1872; married first, Feb. 22, 1827,
Hannah Hall, born Nov. 29, 1805, died March 19, 1832;
married second, —— 1834, Nancy A. Hopkins, born
May 16, 1806, died April 5, 1843; married third, Dec. 6,
1845, Hannah T. Hopkins, born Sept. 23, 1811.

CHILD BY FIRST WIFE.

364 Julia A.[7]   b. Oct. 8, 1828.

CHILDREN BY SECOND WIFE.

365 George F.[7] b. Sept. 15, 1836, d. Oct. 20, 1837.
366 Hannah H.[7] " June 25, 1837. ....
367 Helen M.[7] " May 14, 1839, " Oct. 25, 1841.

CHILDREN BY THIRD WIFE.

368 John F.[7]   b. Oct. 18, 1849, d. July 28, 1873.
369 Evert N.[7] " Sept. 27, 1853, " March 23, 1872.

205.

PRUDENCE CHAPMAN,[6] born ——, died March 1829;
married, Dec. 25, 1777, Samuel Loring of Duxbury,
Mass., born 1736-7, died Oct. 16, 1816.   Duxbury, Mass.,
family.

CHILDREN.

370 Anna[7]   b. Nov. .. 1778,   d. Oct. 25, 1779.
371 Hannah[7]   " May 16, 1780.   ....
372 Benjamin[7]   " Jan. 9, 1784,   " July 2, 1788.
373 Lucy[7]   " Sept. 8, 1790.   ....
374 Prudence[7]   " Aug. 11, 1789.   ....
375 Samuel[7]   " July 17, 1798.   ....

209.

SARAH CHAPMAN,[6] born in Hanover, Mass., ——;
married Joshua Josselyn.   Family removed to state of
Maine.

CHILDREN.

376 Judson[7]   b. .... .. 1789.
377 Ambrose L.[7] " .... .. 1791.   ....
378 Ira L.[7]   " .... .. 1791.
379 Abraham[7]   " .... .. 1793.

210.

MARY CHAPMAN,[6] born in Hanover, Mass; married
Peleg Perry of Pembroke.   Family removed to state of
Maine.

211.

—— CHAPMAN,[6] born in Hanover, Mass; married —— Cushing of Hanover, Mass.

212.

ABIGAIL CHAPMAN,[6] born in Hanover, Mass; married Chester Stoddard of Hingham, Mass. Family removed to state of New York, to some locality unknown to the family now living in Hanover.

214.

RUTH CHAPMAN,[6] born in Hanover, Mass.; married Ephraim Bowen. The family lived in Scipio, N. Y., where Bowen died. There were a number of children, with one of whom Mrs. Bowen was living as late as 1874 in Portland, Michigan.

215.

JOSEPH CHAPMAN,[6] born in Hanover; removed to California; married Hannah Clark of Watertown, Mass.

CHILDREN.

380 Amanda A.[7] ....
381 Melissa[7] ....

216.

DANIEL CHAPMAN,[6] born in Hanover, Mass., Jan. 27, 1800; married, Dec. 12, 1821, Clarissa Burbank, born in Cohasset, Mass., Sept. 15, 1804.

CHILDREN.

382 Clarissa[7]	b. May 8, 1823.	....
383 Harriet[7]	" Nov. 1, 1824.	....
384 Ara[7]	" Oct. 14, 1827,	d. Sept. 1, 1852.
385 Timothy B.[7]	" July 18, 1831.	....
386 Daniel L.[7]	" Sept. 15, 1834.	....
387 Laura A,[7]	" July 24, 1840.	....

217.

EDWIN CHAPMAN,[6] born in Hanover, Mass., April 1802; died 1847 in Mexico, during Mexican war; unmarried.

218.

KILBORN CHAPMAN,[6] born in Hanover, Mass., May 6, 1805, died in Ashby, Mass., Nov. 16, 1865; married 1829, at Medford, Mary Butters, born in Townsend, Mass., Nov. 25, 1809.

CHILDREN.

388 Mary K.[7]	b. June 15, 1830.	....
389 Ruth A.[7]	" Oct. 27, 1832,	d. Dec. 2, 1874.
390 John W.[7]	" Feb. 27, 1835.	....
391 Sarah A.[7]	" March 2, 1839.	
392 Edwin[7]	" April 17, 1841.	
393 Alice M.[7]	" Aug. 6, 1845.	....
394 Eliza[7]	" Nov. 25, 1848,	" Aug. 25, 1851.

220.

BRENTON CHAPMAN,[6] of Newport, R. I.

CHILDREN.

395 Elizabeth[7] b. ...... 1786.
396 Peleg[7] " Dec. 25, 1788.   ....
397 Rebecca[7]   ....
398 Mary[7]

227.

HARRIET A. CHAPMAN,[7] born in Southeast, Putnam
Co., N. Y., Sept. 15, 1795; married first, in 1804, Almon
R. Olmsted, born 1793, died in New Orleans, La., 1807;
married second, Nov. 24, 1825, Daniel Fox, born in W.
Stockbridge, Mass., Sept. 15, 1795, died in Pitcher, N. Y.,
Aug. 22, 1858. Family reside in Sheldon, Pa.

CHILDREN.

399 Juline L.[8] b. Nov. 10, 1827.   ....
400 Oscar C.[8] " Aug. 23, 1830.   ....
401 Aner C.[8] " Nov. 30, 1833, d. Feb. 8, 1849.

111.

ANNA M. CHAPMAN,[7] born in Southeast, N. Y., March
27, 1797, died in Granby, N. Y., April 26, 1863, unmarried

229.

POLLY M. CHAPMAN,[7] born in Southeast, N. Y., Feb.
10, 1799, died in Pitcher, N. Y., June 30, 1870; married,
about 1848, Sylvester K. Cole of Pitcher, N. Y. No
issue.

230.

PETER CHAPMAN,[7] born in Sherburne, N. Y., Feb. 13, 1802, died in Minetto, N. Y., May 10, 1874, unmarried.

231.

CHARLES W. CHAPMAN,[7] born in Sherburne. N. Y., Dec. 17, 1803, died in Smyrna, N. Y., Dec. 27, 1870; married, 1836, widow Nancy Holly (born Browning) born Oct. 1809. No issue.

232.

WILLIAM W. CHAPMAN,[7] born in Sherburne, N. Y., May 8, 1807; married, April 22, 1842, Rebecca Copeland of Carleton, Mass., born Aug. 18, 1820, died in Sherburne, N. Y., Jan. 8, 1843; married, Dec. 24, 1850, Hannah Dixon, born in Sherburne, N. Y., Aug. 28, 1826. Family reside in Sarpy Centre, Sarpy Co., Nebraska.

CHILDREN.

402 Isaac P.[8]   b. Dec. 20, 1851.   . . . .
403 William D.[8] " Oct. 23, 1853.   . . . .
404 Harriet[8]   " Sept. 4, 1855,   d. Sept. 30, 1861.
405 Pike W.[8]   " Nov. 18, 1858.   . . . .
406 Olive[8]   " July 15, 1864.   . . . .

233.

LUCIUS LYSANDER CHAPMAN,[7] born in Sherburne, N. Y., Oct. 30, 1809; married, March 26, 1835, Jerusha Hutchinson of Smyrna, N. Y., born Aug. 2, 1814, died

in Sherburne May 2, 1849; married, Nov. 29, 1849, Fidelia Loomis of Bolton, Conn. Family reside in Earl-
ville, Madison county, N. Y.

CHILDREN.
407 Clarrisa[8] b. Feb. 16, 1840.   ....
408 Stark[8]   " Jan. 15, 1842.   ....
409 Kate[8]   " March 17, 1849.   ....

234.

HANNAH CHAPMAN,[7] born in Sherburne, N. Y., Aug.
30, 1811; married, 1848, James Kennedy, born ——, died
in Plattford, Neb., 1873. Plattford, Neb., family.

CHILD.
410 Sarah J.[8]   b. May 8, 1849.   ....

235.

EMMA JANE CHAPMAN,[7] born in New Lisbon, N. Y.,
July 18, 1817; married, Oct, 10, 1838, Joel Lee, born in
Sherburne, N. Y., Feb. 19, 1816, died in Hannibal, N. Y.,
Jan. 9, 1865. Family reside in Milford, Ill.

CHILDREN.
411 Ann[8]   b. Dec. 5, 1840.
412 Alson[8]   " Aug. 1, 1842.   ....
413 Wells[8]   " Feb. 12, 1848,   d. Sept. 12, 1873.
414 Nettie[8]   " Sept. 8, 1850.   ....
415 Charles[8]   " March 29, 1855, " March 5, 1867.

236.

LAURA L. CHAPMAN,[7] born in Butternuts, Otsego Co.,

N. Y., Oct. 8, 1819; married, Sept. 14, 1859, Marcus N.
Wadsworth, born in Framingham, Conn., Feb. 27, 1806,
died Sept. 28, 1867, in Oswego, N. Y. No issue. Mrs.
Wadsworth resides in Minetto, N. Y.

245.

LORENZO CHAPMAN,[7] born May 18, 1810; married first,
May 13, 1835, Lavina Hatch, born April 13, 1817, died
in Amity, Pa., about 1845; married second, Dolly Hatch,
born March 10, 1822, died about 1852; married third,
Feb. 22, 1852, Mary Sears, born March 15, 1834. Family
reside in Mina, Chatauque Co., N. Y.

CHILDREN BY FIRST WIFE.

416	Emily[8]	b. Sept. 12, 1836,	d.	. . . .
417	Eli H.[8]	" Aug. 17, 1838.		. . . .
418	Alonzo W.[8]	" July 26, 1840,	"	. . . . . . 1868.
419	Ruhannah J[8]	" Aug. 20, 1842,	"	"
420	Lavina M.[8]	" July 23, 1834,	"	. . . . . . "

CHILDREN BY SECOND WIFE.

421	Silas E.[8]	b. Dec. 25, 1846.	. . . .
422	Isaac E.[8]	" Jan. 6, 1849.	. . . .
423	Lamont V.[8]	" May 17, 1850.	. . . .

CHILDREN BY THIRD WIFE.

424	Mary S.[8]	b. Nov. 2, 1855.	. . . .
425	George F.[8]	" Sept. 3, 1857.	. . . .
426	Ora L.[8]	" June 22, 1859.	. . . .
427	Vincent W.[8]	" Jan. 21, 1861.	. . . .

428 Mina[8]   b. Sept. 23, 1864.   . . . .
429 Idell E.[8]   " Sept. 9, 1866.

247.

MINERVA CHAPMAN,[7] born Sept. 10, 1819, died in Northeast, Pa., June 2, 1848; married, Jan. 5, 1841, John Sillyman of Northeast, Pa., born July 5, 1804. Family reside near Northeast, Pa.

CHILDREN.

430 Mary A.[8]   b. June 18, 1842. . . . .
431 James E.[8]   " June 10, 1844. . . . .
432 Sarah H.[8] " May 28, 1846. . . . .

248.

DELINDA CHAPMAN,[7] born ———, died about 1867: married Jeremiah Ordway of ———.

CHILDREN.

433 Name unknown. . . . .
434   "   "   . . . .
435   "   "   . . . .
436   "   "   . . . .
437   "   "   '. . . . .

249.

LIVONIA ADELINE CHAPMAN,[7] born in Cincinnatus, N.Y., June 5, 1810, died April 18, 1845; married, Jan. 15, 1838, Ethan Sherwin, born May 4, 1796, died in Great Valley, N. Y., Jan. 6, 1874. Friendship, N. Y., family.

CHILDREN.

438 Sarah M.[8]   b. Oct. 26, 1838.   . . . .
439 Caroline V.[8] " March 10, 1841.
440 Livonia A.[8] " April 23, 1843.
441 Addison M.[8] " April 11, 1845.

250.

LEANDER F. CHAPMAN,[7] born in Cazenovia, N. Y., Sept. 26, 1812; married, Dec. 20, 1835, Hannah Kirkpatrick, born in Oriel, N. Y., Dec. 19, 1812. Friendship, N. Y., family.

CHILDREN.

442 John K.[8]   b. Oct 4, 1836.   . . . .
443 Elvira L.[8]   " Sept. 13, 1841.   . . . .
444 Laura May[8] " May 5, 1848.
445 Harrison S.[8] " Sept. 18, 1849.   . . . .

251.

MARGETTA C. CHAPMAN,[7] born in Jerusalem N. Y., Nov. 13, 1818; married, Dec. 21, 1835, Cyrus Lewis, born June 2, 1816. Dearbornville, Ill., family.

CHILDREN.

446 Ellen L.[8]   b. March 23, 1838, d. August 4, 1841.
447 Arvilla A.[8]   " Feb. 20, 1840.   . . . .
448 Martha E.[8]   " June 26, 1842.   . . . .
449 Velorous C.[8] " July 20, 1844.   . . . .
450 Alice G.[8]   " July 23, 1846.   . . . .
451 Laura E.[8]   " April 1, 1849.   . . . .

452 Henry F.[8] b. July 3, 1854, d. Oct. 16, 1855.
453 Frances M.[8] " April 11, 1859.

253.

J. Addison Chapman,[7] born in Friendship, N. Y.,
Sept. 4, 1821; married first, May 16, 1849, Phebe Lang
of Tyrone, N. Y., born 1830, died Oct. 17, 1860; married
second, Nov. 30, 1861, Mary J. Kenyon of Dundee, born
1839, died Sept. 27, 1869; married third, May 18, 1871,
Anna F. Hartlieb of Portland, Oregon. Family reside
in Portland, Oregon.

CHILDREN BY FIRST WIFE.
454 Frank H.[8] b. April 11, 1850, d. Sept. 15, 1852.
455 Addison L.[8] " Nov. 16, 1853, " Oct. 9, 1855.
456 William L.[8] " Sept. 4, 1859. . . . .
CHILDREN BY SECOND WIFE.
457 Lena May[8] b. Oct. 24, 1862. . . . .
458 James H.[8] " May 6, 1864. . . . .
CHILD BY THIRD WIFE.
459 Anna F.[8] b. Oct. 8, 1872, d. June 24, 1873.

254.

Laura K. Chapman,[7] born April 1, 1826, in Friend-
ship, N. Y., married, Sept. 30, 1847, Russell Sandford of
Wayne, N. Y., born Nov. 15, 1822. Family reside in
Wayne, N. Y.

CHILDREN.
460 Emma R.[8] b. May 10, 1850 . . . .
461 Mary E.[8] " March 21, 1853. . . . .

283.

MARY E. CHAPMAN,[7] born in Newburgh, N. Y., March 16, 1821; married, Sept. 30, 1839, William H. Gerard, born in Newburgh, N. Y., April 13, 1815, died in Poughkeepsie, N. Y., May 1, 1876 Newburgh, N. Y., family.

CHILDREN.

462	William R.[8]	b. March 29, 1841.	....
463	John N.[8]	" Aug. 21, 1843.	....
464	Charles B.[8]	" Oct. 19, 1845.	....
465	Edward C.[8]	" Oct. 14, 1847.	....
466	James C.[8]	" April 29, 1850.	....
467	Frank W.[8]	" Feb. 14, 1853.	....
468	Henri[8]	" Nov. 10, 1855.	....
469	Mary L.[8]	" Dec. 12, 1857.	d. Nov. 11, 1860.
470	Frederick K[8]	" March 22, 1860.	" June 21, 1861.
471	George[8]	" Aug. 8, 1862,	" July 1, 1863.

284.

JOSEPH H. H. CHAPMAN,[7] born in Newburgh, N. Y., March 12, 1823; married, Sept. 20, 1848, Lydia W., daughter of Edmund Sanxay of Newburgh, born Sept. 7, 1826, died March 31, 1876. Family reside in Newburgh, N. Y.

CHILDREN.

472	Maria H.[8]	b. Sept. 16, 1849.	....
473	Davenport S[8]	" Jan. 1, 1852,	d. May 12, 1853.
474	Euphemia V[8]	" Aug. 18, 1854,	" May 31, 1872.

475 Joseph H.* b. Oct. 29, 1856.
476 Francis E.* " March 3, 1859.   ....,........
477 John S.* " May 23, 1866, d. April 9, 1873.
478 George F.* " June 7, 1869.   ....

285.

CATHARINE M. CHAPMAN,[7] born December 1, 1824; unmarried; resides in Laporte, Indiana.

286.

SUSAN A. CHAPMAN,[7] born in Newburgh, N. Y., Feb. 2, 1827; married, May 25, 1852, Ithamar D. Phelps, born in Missisquoi, Canada East, Feb. 7, 1822. Family reside in Laporte, Ind.

CHILDREN.

479 Mary L.[8]   b. Jan. 25, 1855.   ....,
480 William G.[8] " April 29, 1858.   ....

287.

DEBORAH A. CHAPMAN,[7] born March 9, 1829; unmarried; resides in Newburgh, N. Y.

288.

THOMAS P. CHAPMAN,[7] born in Newburgh, N. Y., June 1, 1831; married, Dec. 15, 1852, Lydia Crist, born Aug. 30, 1830. Family reside in Newburgh, N. Y.

CHILDREN.

481 Mary E.[8]   b. March 12, 1854.   ....

482 Louise[8]   b. Jan. 8, 1861..   . . . .

483 Emma H.[8]   " March 31, 1865.   . . . .

289.

ISAAC C. CHAPMAN,[7] born in Newburgh, N. Y., July 31, 1833; married, April 10, 1856, Letitia Kennedy, born in Newburgh, N. Y., Aug. 22, 1834. Family reside in Newburgh, N. Y.

CHILD.

484 John H.[8]   b. Feb. 1, 1860.   . . . .

290.

CHARLES F. CHAPMAN,[7] born in Newburgh, N. Y., Aug. 5, 1835; married, Oct. 15, 1861, Agnes Hamilton, born in Newburgh, N. Y., Jan. 18, 1840. Family reside in Newburgh, N. Y.

CHILDREN.

485 Charles F.[8] b. Nov. 13, 1862.   . . . .

486 Frank G.[8]   " Jan. 3, 1867.   . . . .

292.

WILLIAM G. CHAPMAN,[7] born in Newburgh, N. Y., Nov. 16, 1839; married, April 21, 1869, Emmeline Welch, born in Brooklyn, N. Y., Jan. 5, 1845. Family reside in Peekskill, N. Y.

CHILDREN.

487 Mary L.[8]   b. Jan. 30, 1870.   . . . .

488 Sarah E.[8]   " Dec. 14, 1872.   . . . .

489 Ralph[8]   " May 22, 1874,   d. Feb. 28, 1875.

293.

CAROLINE G. CHAPMAN,[7] born in Newburgh, N. Y., Dec. 21, 1842; married, Nov. 9, 1864, Henry Hunter, born in Newburgh Jan. 16, 1838. Family reside in Newburgh, N. Y.

CHILDREN.

490 William G.[8] b. Aug. 19, 1865.
491 Carrie S.[8] " April 23, 1870.

298.

WILLIAM E. CHAPMAN,[7] born in New York City Sept. 22, 1832; married, Aug. 31, 1859, Lucinda F. Budd, born in New York City July 30, 1841. Family reside in Brooklyn, N. Y.

CHILDREN.

492 Isaac E.[8] b. March 17, 1861.
493 Frances H.[8] " Jan. 21, 1863. . . . .
494 William L.[8] " Jan. 28, 1866. . . . .
495 Alfred N.[8] " May 4, 1874. . . . .

299.

ALONZO R. CHAPMAN,[7] born April 14, 1834; married first, Aug. 16, 1859, Nancy J. Hewitt, born May 1, 1840, died July 1, 1864; married second, Oct. 11, 1866, Sarah E. Welch, born March 28, 1843. Family reside in Peekskill, N. Y.

CHILDREN BY FIRST WIFE.

496 Sarah E.[8] b. May 24, 1860 . . . .
497 William H.[8] " Sept. 30, 1863. . . . .

CHILDREN BY SECOND WIFE.

498 Carrie E.[8]   b. Feb. 11, 1869.   ....
499 George A.[8] " July 28, 1870.
500 John F.[8]   " Nov. 9, 1872.   ....

309.

LOIS H. CHAPMAN,[7] born in Dennis, Mass., April 30, 1835; married first, Aug. 27, 1861, Thaddeus Crosby of Dennis, died in Shanghai, China, Oct. 12, 1862; married second, Nov. 17, 1869, Daniel H. Robbins of Dennis, Mass., born Feb. 3, 1837. Family reside in Dennis.

CHILDREN.

501 Lois C.[8]   b. Jan. 20, 1871.   ....
502 Daniel C.[8] " Jan. 12, 1872.   ....

310.

· SAMUEL CHAPMAN,[7] born in Dennis, Mass, March 6, 1837; married, Feb. 1, 1868, Lydia C. Hall, born in Barnstead. N. H., Aug. 1, 1847. Family reside in Dennis, Mass.

CHILDREN.

503 Helen F.[8]   b. Dec. 2, 1871.   ....
504 Sophronia L.[8] " Aug. 27, 1873.

313.

SOPHRONIA H. CHAPMAN,[7] born in Dennis, Mass., March 29, 1847; married, Jan. 3, 1867, Joshua Crowell, born in Dennis, Mass., Oct. 24, 1843. Family reside in Dennis, Mass.

CHILDREN.

505 Olive H.[8]   b. Sept. 6, 1869.
506 Seth[8]   " March 13, 1872.

316.

MINERVA H. CHAPMAN,[7] born in Dennis, Mass., July 23, 1843; married, May 27, 1869, Luther Hall, born in Dennis, Mass., Nov. 5, 1843. Family reside in Dennis.

CHILDREN.

507 Frank B.[8]   b. Nov. 25, 1870.   ....
508 Joseph S.[8]   " April 11, 1873,   d. April 21, 1874.

318.

NELSON S. CHAPMAN,[7] born in Dennis, Mass., April 25, 1847; married, Jan. 18, 1870, Rebecca Hall, born in Dennis, Nov. 3, 1849. Lives in Dennis.

330.

REUBEN A. CHAPMAN,[7] born in Dennis, Mass., Aug. 6, 1807; married, Jan. 11, 1831, Caroline Loomis, born Oct. 20, 1808. E. Hartford, Conn., family.

CHILDREN.

509 John H.[8]   b. Oct. 26, 1833,   d. Jan. 18, 1834.
510 Mary A.[8]   " April 18, 1835.   ....
511 John W.[8]   " Aug. 26, 1837.   ....
512 Harriet B.[8] " Jan. 20, 1839,   " April 22, 1873.
513 Caroline[8]   " Sept. 27, 1848.   ....

331.

CALVIN CHAPMAN,[7] born Oct. 22, 1810, died Dec. 11,

1839; married, ——, Mary K. Smith, born Sept. 3, 1812.

CHILDREN.

514 George[8]   b. Aug. 6, 1833.
515 Reuben[8]   " Dec. 6, 1834.
516 Abbie[8]   " Aug. 3, 1836.   ....

333.

EBEN P. CHAPMAN,[7] born July 6, 1815; married, Jan. 20, 1850, Harriet Knowles, born July 1, 1816. Family reside in Brewster, Mass.

CHILDREN.

517 Harriet A.[8] b. Dec. 10, 1851,   d. Aug. 23, 1852.
518 Reuben[8]   " May 1, 1853.   ....
519 Joseph C.[8] " Aug. 21, 1854.   ....

334.

JAMES CHAPMAN,[7] born in Dennis, Mass., March 7, 1810, died in Barnstable, Mass., Oct. 10, 1856; married, Dec. 1, 1831, Anna J. D. Higgins, born in Eastham, Mass., April 4, 1810, died in Barnstable, Mass., March 7, 1866.

CHILDREN.

520 Mary A.[8]   b. Nov. 2, 1832,   d. April 8, 1861.
521 James H.[8]   " Nov. 21, 1834.   ....
522 Hannah W.[8] " May 31, 1836.   ....
523 Bennet W.[8] " Sept. 3, 1838,   " July 25, 1839.
524 John F.[8]   " May 22, 1840,   " Nov. 22, 1865.
525 Martha G.[8] " Feb. 26, 1842,   " Nov. 12, 1865.

526 Mercy J.[8]   b. Nov. 26, 1844,   d. Oct. 13, 1861.
527 Phebe H.[8]   " Nov. 21, 1846,   " June 22, 1864.
528 Pamelia B.[8] " March 9, 1849,   " Jan. 9, 1855.
529 Sarah E.[8]   " Aug. 6, 1852.   ....
530 Catherine L[8] " Feb. 21, 1855.   ....

335.

HENRY CHAPMAN,[7] born in Dennis, Mass., Oct. 22, 1811; married, April 27, 1837, Martha D. Green, born June 26, 1811.

CHILDREN.

531 Henry T.G.[8] b. June 9, 1838.   ....
532 Walter[8]   " Aug. 27, 1840,   d. May 25, 1865.
533 Martha G.[8] " March 19, 1845.   ....

336.

PAMELIA CHAPMAN,[7] born Sept. 20, 1813; married first, Nov. 17, 1833, Alexander Baker, born May 23, 1809, died July 7, 1846; married second, Jan. 1, 1868, William Oliver of South Yarmouth, Mass.

CHILDREN.

534 Pamelia M.[8] b. Oct. 27, 1836,   d. March 1, 1861.
535 Alexander[8]   " July 12, 1844.   ....
536 Charles G.[8] " May 10, 1846.   ....

337.

MARY CHAPMAN,[7] born July 10, 1815, died July 10, 1854; married, Nov. 4, 1834, William D. Burgess of Cambridgeport, Mass., born Aug. 12, 1812.

CHILDREN.

537 William H.⁸ b. Sept. 23, 1835.   ....
538 Mary E.⁸   " Jan. 11, 1840,   d. April 14, 1852.
539 Caroline⁸   " Nov. 17, 1842,   " March 9, 1859.
540 Albert L.⁸   " April 7, 1845.   ....

347.

NATHAN CHAPMAN,⁷ born in Dennis, Mass., July 11, 1821; married, Dec. 2, 1852, Fannie Roxanna Paine, born Feb. 23, 1824. Family reside in Lincoln, Nebraska.

CHILDREN.

541 Nathaniel P⁸ b. Nov. 20, 1853,   d. Sept. 7, 1854.
542 Austin F.⁸   " July 25, 1858,   " April 10, 1864.

348.

DAVID S. CHAPMAN,⁷ born in Dennis, Mass., Dec. 30, 1822; married Sallie E. Sears. No issue.

349.

ELIZA A. CHAPMAN,⁷ born in Dennis, Mass., March 15, 1824; married, Feb. 25, 1845, Alexander Robbins, born Jan. 19, 1818. Family reside in St. Louis, Mo.

CHILDREN.

543 AlexanderH⁸b. Feb. 22, 1846.   ....
544 Edmund H.⁸ " March 25, 1849.   ....
545 Nelson C.⁸ " May 8, 1851.
546 Charles C.⁸ " Jan. 15, 1854.
547 Lurin C.⁸   " Oct. 14, 1859.
548 Cyrus⁸   " Feb. 17, 1863.   ....

350.

BENJAMIN F. CHAPMAN,[7] born in Dennis, Mass., Jan. 21, 1826; married, Nov. 29, 1849, Sallie Crowell, born July 23, 1828. Family reside in Brocton, Mass.

CHILDREN.

549 E. Addie[8]   b. Sept. 26, 1850.   . . . .
550 Isaac C.[8]   " March 6, 1856.
551 Benjamin[8]   " Dec. 13, 1864.

352.

MARY F. CHAPMAN,[7] born in Dennis, Mass., May 1, 1829; married Miller Whelden, born ———, died April 21, 1862.

CHILDREN.

552 Eliza J.[8]   b. Dec. 16, 1849.   . . . .
553 George M.[8]   " Sept. 28, 1851.   . . . .
554 William M.[8] " July 11, 1854.   . . . .

353.

HARRIET N. CHAPMAN,[7] born in Dennis, Mass., Jan. 9, 1832; married, Feb. 9, 1854, Rowland Howes.

CHILDREN.

555 Isaiah[8]   b. Dec. 30, 1854.   . . . .
556 Charles F.[8]   " Aug. 13, 1856.   . . . .
557 Hattie May[8] " Sept. 5, 1863.   . . . .

354.

GEORGE B. CHAPMAN,[7] born in Dennis, Mass., Jan. 4,

1834, died at sea Jan. 10, 1871; married, Oct. 23, 1862, Nancy C. Sears.

CHILD.

558 George C.[8] b. Feb. 15, 1865. ....

355.

HORATIO CHAPMAN,[7] born in Dennis, Mass., Jan. 30, 1837; married, May 9, 1866, Mary E. Smith of Harwich, Mass., born Oct. 23, 1841. Family reside in Dennisport, Mass.

CHILDREN.

559 Ida M.[8]   b. Oct. 4, 1867   ....
560 Horatio F.[8]   " June 7, 1870.   ....
561 Maletta L.[8]   " Oct. 25, 1872.   ....

356.

CHARLES C. CHAPMAN,[7] born in Dennis, Mass., April 29, 1842; married, Nov. 29, 1866, Christina M. Fairfield, born May 9, 1842. Family reside in S. Boston, Mass.

CHILDREN.

562 Charles[8]   b. Oct. 4, 1867.   ....
563 Mabel C.[8]   " Nov. 3, 1872.   ....
564 ——[8]   " June 12, 1874.

357.

ABRAHAM CHAPMAN,[7] born in Dennis, Mass., March 9, 1828; married Phebe Clark of Brewster, Mass. Family reside in Dennis, Mass.

CHILDREN.

565 Frederick C.[8] b. Oct. 25, 1859. . . . .
566 Alfred G.[8] " Sept. 30, 1862. . . . .
567 Etta Luella[8] " April 13, 1870.
568 Carrie L.[8] " May 25, 1872. . . . .

358.

EUNICE H. CHAPMAN,[7] born in Dennis, Mass., June 16, 1836; married Levi Chase, born April 1, 1836.

CHILD.

569 Levi R.[8]   b. Oct. 19, 1873. . . . .

364.

JULIA A. CHAPMAN,[7] born in Dennis, Mass., Oct. 8, 1828; married, Oct. 24, 1860, Porter O. Kent, born in Compton, Canada East, March 3, 1837. Family reside in Candia, N. H.

CHILD.

570 Porter O.[8] b. Sept. 7, 1868. . . . .

366.

HANNAH H. CHAPMAN,[7] born in Dennis, Mass., June 25, 1837; married, Nov. 27, 1875, Jesse M. Rhodes. Reside in Lynn, Mass.

380.

AMANDA CHAPMAN,[7] daughter of Joseph Chapman of Hanover, Mass.; married first, William Mathiott; married second, Thomas Blackmore of Boston, Mass.

381.

MELISSA CHAPMAN,[7] daughter of Joseph Chapman of Hanover, Mass.; married John C. Bull of Boston, Mass.

382.

CLARISSA CHAPMAN,[7] born in Quincy, Mass., May 8, 1823; married, Sept. 15, 1844, William F. Harris, born in Baintree, Mass., March 18, 1822. Family reside in South Scittuate, Mass.

CHILDREN.

571 William F.[8]	b. May 7, 1846.		. . . .
572 Clara S.[8]	" May 27, 1848,	d. Aug. 18, 1850.	
573 Charles W.[8]	" Oct. 4, 1851,	" Aug. 8, 1852.	
574 Clara Alice[8]	" July 26, 1853.		. . . .
575 Mary Louisa[8]	" June 4, 1855,	" Jan. 4, 1859.	
576 Laura F.[8]	" March 16, 1857.		. . . .

383.

HARRIET CHAPMAN,[7] born in Hanover, Mass., Nov. 1, 1824; married, July 19, 1843, Laban Wilder, born in Hingham, Mass. Family reside in S. Scittuate, Mass.

CHILDREN.

577 Harriet M.[8]	b. July 20, 1845,	d. May 27, 1847.
578 Harriet M.[8]	" Jan. 18, 1848.	. . . .
579 Emma D.[8]	" Oct. 10, 1851.	. . . .
580 George N.[8]	" Nov. 19, 1855.	. . . .
581 William E.[8]	" Nov. 5, 1857.	. . . .

384.

ARA CHAPMAN,[7] born in Hanover, Mass., Oct. 14, 1827, died in Hanover Sept. 1, 1852; married, March 1851, Sarah W. Damon of Hanover.

CHILD.

582 Eugene L.[8] b. Sept. 10, 1851. ....

385.

TIMOTHY B. CHAPMAN,[7] born in Hanover, Mass., July 18, 1831 ; married, Dec. 25, 1853, Hannah B. Vining, born in Hanover, Sept. 5, 1835.

CHILD.

583 Charles Victor[8] b. April 26, 1856. ....

386.

DANIEL L. CHAPMAN,[7] born in Hanover, Mass., Sept. 15, 1834; married, Dec. 27, 1860, Fidelia W. Raymond of East Weymouth, Mass., born June 15, 1844, died Dec. 7, 1874, in Hanover.

CHILDREN.

584 Edward E.[8] b. March 26, 1861.
585 Lillie May[8] " May 22, 1866. ....
586 Ara B.[8] " Dec. 14, 1871, d. March 2, 1872.

387.

LAURA A. CHAPMAN,[7] born in Hanover, Mass., July 24, 1840; married, Oct. 1857, Elias V. Raymond of East

Weymouth, Mass., born July 6, 1837.   East Weymouth family.

CHILDREN.

587 Lloyd A.⁸   b. Jan. 11, 1859.   ....
588 Clara Isola⁸ " May 13, 1867.   ....

388.

MARY K. CHAPMAN,⁷ born in Charlestown, Mass., June 15, 1830; married, June 13, 1850, Richard H. Ingalls of Charlestown, born ——, died in Boston, Mass., April 26, 1857.

CHILD.

589 Augustus H.⁸ b. June 14, 1851, d. Oct. 12, 1853.

389.

RUTH A. CHAPMAN,⁷ born in Charlestown, Mass., Oct. 27, 1832, died Dec. 2, 1874; married first, May 21, 1855, William S. Williams, born in Alstead, N. H., died in Charlestown, Mass., Nov. 26, 1866; married second, April 26, 1867, Lucius Sias of Charlestown.   No issue.

390.

JOHN W. CHAPMAN,⁷ born in Charlestown, Mass., Feb. 27, 1835; married, Aug. 5, 1855, Catherine A. Paine, born ——, died in South Boston, Mass., March 1865.

CHILD.

590 Mary J.⁸   b. July 3, 1857.   ....

391.

SARAH A. CHAPMAN,[7] born in Brighton, Mass., March 2, 1839; married, Nov. 3, 1864, Andrew J. Lavery of Boston, Mass.

CHILDREN.

591 Edward A.[8] b. July 24, 1865. ....
592 Alice J.[8] " Dec. 6, 1867. ....

392.

EDWIN CHAPMAN,[7] born in Cambridgeport, Mass., April 17, 1841; married, Oct. 27, 1864, Mary P. Hubbard, born in Ashby, Mass., Nov. 23, 1845. Family reside in Charlestown, Mass.

CHILDREN.

593 Mary G.[8] b. Aug. 3, 1866. ....
594 Georgia L.[8] " Feb. 23, 1868. ....
595 Alonzo E.[8] " Dec. 31, 1869, d. Oct. 1, 1870.
596 Florence A.[8] " Sept. 18, 1872. ....

393.

ALICE M. CHAPMAN,[7] born in Sudbury, Mass., Aug. 6, 1845; married, Dec. 31, 1863, Levi Kenerson of Hingham, Mass. Family reside in South Boston, Mass.

CHILDREN.

597 Alice M.[8] b. March 3, 1865, d. Sept. 29, 1865.
598 Ella M.[8] " Feb. 2, 1866. ....
599 Grace E.[8] " Aug. 5, 1868. ....
600 Carrie A.[8] " June 23, 1870. ....

396.

PELEG CHAPMAN,[7] born in Newport, Rhode Island, Dec. 25, 1788.*

CHILDREN.

601 William B.[8] ....
602 Rebecca K.[8] .... d. .... 1875.
603 Mary[8] ....
604 Name unknown.
605 " ..
606 " "
607 " ..
608 " " ....

402.

ISAAC P. CHAPMAN,[8] born in Sherburne, N. Y., Dec. 20, 1851; married, Jan. 27, 1874, Cynthia Jennie Hazen, born in Portage City, Wis., Aug. 22, 1856. Family reside in Sarpy Centre, Nebraska.

CHILDREN.

609 Pike N.[9] b. Oct. 28, 1874.
610 William V.[9] " Sept. 22, 1875. ....

407.

CLARRISA CHAPMAN,[8] born in Smyrna, N. Y., Feb. 16, 1840; married, Oct. 18, 1866, Harvey L. Horton, born in Stockbridge, N. Y., April 26, 1837. No issue. Reside in Stockbridge, N. Y.

---

* The record of this family was promised me by the last surviving member of it, but who died before fulfilling her promise.—*C. B. G.*

442.

JOHN K. CHAPMAN,[8] born in Friendship, N. Y., Oct, 4, 1836; married, Jan. 5, 1859, Mary E. Williams, born in Albany, N. Y., Feb. 23, 1840. Family reside in Hornellsville, N. Y.

CHILD.

611 Sarah L.[9] b. Nov. 3, 1859. . . . .

443.

ELVIRA L. CHAPMAN,[8] born in Cuba, N. Y., Sept. 13, 1841; married. Sept. 5, 1866, Thomas C. Smith, born in Williamsport, Pa., June 5, 1844. Family reside in Portland, Oregon.

CHILDREN.

612 Laura May[9] b. Oct. 14, 1867.
613 James A.[9] " Oct. 17, 1869. . . . .
614 Thomas C.[9] " Jan. 15, 1872. . . . .

445.

HARRISON S. CHAPMAN,[8] born in Belvidere, N. Y., Sept. 18, 1849; married, June 8, 1871, Florence J. Hendershott, born in Hornellsville, N. Y., March 13, 1851. Family reside in Buffalo, N. Y.

CHILDREN.

615 Harry A.[9] b. May 20, 1872, d. May 31, 1872.
616 Laura B.[9] " Jan. 8, 1874. . . . .

472.

MARIA H. CHAPMAN,[8] born in Newburgh, N. Y., Sept.

16, 1849; married, April 27, 1870, Robert Whitehill, born in Glasgow, Scotland, June 1, 1845. Family reside in Newburgh, N. Y.

CHILDREN.

617 Robert C.[9] b. May 13, 1871. . . . .
618 Effie C.[9] " June 6, 1873.
618ª Walter H.[9] " Feb. 20, 1876. . . . .

510.

MARY A. CHAPMAN,[8] born April 18, 1835; married, Jan. 14, 1862, Frederick F. Street of East Hartford, Conn., born Jan. 26, 1829. No issue. East Hartford, Conn., family.

ADOPTED CHILD.

621 Hattie May* b. March 29, 1873 . . . .

511.

JOHN W. CHAPMAN,[3] born Aug. 26, 1837; married, Feb. 20, 1873, Mary C. Dimon, born Sept. 20, 1852. Family reside in Brooklyn, N. Y.

CHILD.

619 Sarah C.[9] b. April 17, 1874. . . . .

512.

HARRIET B. CHAPMAN,[8] of East Hartford, Conn., born Jan. 20, 1839, died April 22, 1873; married, Oct. 20, 1870, Louis L. Thurwachter of Syracuse, N. Y., born in Freckenfeld, Germany, Sept. 3, 1837.

---
* Daughter of Harriet B. and Louis L. Thurwachter of Syracuse.

CHILDREN.
620 Reuben C.⁹ b. Sept. 30, 1871.   ....
621 Hattie May⁹ " March 29, 1873.   ....

513.

CAROLINE CHAPMAN,⁸ born Sept. 27, 1848; married, 1869, Charles F. Hanmer. Family reside in Burnside, Conn.

CHILDREN.
622 Charles C.⁹ b. Dec. 8. 1869.   ....
623 Carrie⁹   " June 15, 1871,   d. Aug. 15, 1871.
624 Francis⁹   " Aug. 30, 1872.

514.

GEORGE CHAPMAN,⁸ born Aug. 6, 1833, died at sea ——; married, Jan. 1858, Susan G. Higgins.

CHILDREN.
625 Mary G.⁹   b. Aug. 4, 1864.   ....
626 George C.⁹ " Nov. .. 1866, ...

515.

REUBEN CHAPMAN,⁸ born Dec. 6, 1834; married, Aug. 1. 1859, Rebecca A. Arey, born April 11, 1840. Family reside in South Boston, Mass.

CHILD.
627 Flora E.⁹   b. Oct. 5, 1863..   ....

516.

ABBIE CHAPMAN,⁸ born Aug. 3, 1836; married, May

31. 1858, Jesse F. Houghton, born Jan. 11, 1834.   Family
reside in Jamaica Plain, Mass.

CHILDREN.

628 Georgie F.⁹ b. June 8, 1862,   d. July 11, 1869.
629 Fannie F.⁹   " Aug. 10, 1863.   . . . .
630 Albert R.⁹   " Oct. 2, 1865.   . . . .

520.

MARY A. CHAPMAN,⁸ born in Barnstable, Mass., Nov.
2, 1832, died in Plymouth, Mass., April 8, 1861; married,
Aug. 17, 1852, Isaac J. Lucas, born in Plymouth, Mass.,
Feb. 20, 183–, died in Plymouth, Oct. 17, 1858.

CHILD.

631 Jane H.⁹   b. May 14, 1856.   . . . .

521.

JAMES H. CHAPMAN,⁸ born in Barnstable, Mass., Nov.
21, 1834; married, March 27, 1859, Mary B. Dimon of
Plymouth, Mass.   Family reside in Plymouth.

CHILDREN.

632 Mary B.⁹   b. Nov. 8, 1859.   . . . .
633 Walter F.⁹   " Nov. 12, 1862,   d. June 30, 1863.
634 John H.⁹   " Oct. 31, 1864.   . . . .
635 James⁹   " June 17, 1866,   " Aug. 4, 1866.
636 William M.⁹   " Oct. 3, 1868.   . . . .
637 FrederickW⁹   " Dec. 1, 1869,   " July 26, 1870.
638 Edward D.⁹   " Feb. 1, 1871,   " Aug. 12, 1871.
639 George G.⁹   " April 17, 1873, " July 31, 1873.
640 Ralph G.⁹   " Sept. 4, 1874,   " Feb. 8, 1875.

522.

HANNAH W. CHAPMAN,[8] born in Barnstable, Mass., May 31, 1836; married, March 16, 1865, Isaac A. Penney of Lexington, Mass., born Jan. 17, 1826.

CHILD.

641 Thomas H.[9] b. Oct. 25, 1867.

525.

MARTHA G. CHAPMAN,[8] born in Barnstable, Mass., Feb. 26, 1842, died in Plymouth, Mass., Nov. 12, 1865; married, May 26, 1862, Henry Fessenden of Sandwich, Mass.

CHILDREN.

642 Harriet J.[9] b. Sept. .. 1862. . . . .
643 Nannie F.[9] " Nov. 4, 1864. d. Aug. 15, 1865.

531.

HENRY T. G. CHAPMAN,[8] born June 9, 1838; married, Feb. 4, 1863, Mercy Paine, born Feb. 6, 1838. Family reside in Charlestown, Mass.

CHILDREN.

644 Emma F.[9] b. March 18, 1864, d. March 23, 1864.
645 Bertha D.[9] " June 3, 1865. . . . .
646 Martha D.[9] " Feb. 28, 1867. . . . .
647 Edith A.[9] " April 16, 1870. . . . .
648 Walter H.[9] " June 5, 1873, " Sept. 18, 1873.

532.

WALTER CHAPMAN,[a] born Aug. 27, 1840, was killed by explosion of U. S. ordnance in Mobile, Alabama, May 25, 1865; died unmarried.

549.

E. ADDIE CHAPMAN,[a] of Brocton, Mass., born Sept. 26, 1850; married, Nov. 25, 1873, John M. Packard, born Feb. 15, 1846.

APPENDIX.

Descendants of John Chapman.

NOTE.—I have been unable to discover the antecedents of JOHN CHAPMAN, of whose descendants
the records are given below. From careful examination
of old deeds and wills in possession of the family, I have
concluded that he was probably a grandson of John
Chapman, born May 12, 1681—No. 22 in foregoing
records. On account of the uncertainty in regard to
the connection of the families here given with the descendants of Ralph Chapman, they are placed by them-
selves.—C. B. G.

The children of JOHN CHAPMAN* were, as far as
known, as follows:

1	John	b. ... .. 1793.	living in 1875.
2	William	....	....
3	Elizabeth	....	

* He had a brother named Peter.

I.

JOHN CHAPMAN, born 1793, living in 1875 in Tewks-
bury, Mass.   His wife was Elizabeth Hewitt, born 1796,
died in Taunton, Mass., May 19, 1861.

CHILDREN.

4 Sabina	b.	1815.		. . . .
5 Hiram	"	1817.		. . . .
6 Daniel	"	1819,	d. July 2, 1823.	
7 Rebecca	"	1821,	"	1823.
8 Catherine	"	1823.		. . . .
9 Andrew	"	1826.		. . . .
10 Mary J.	"	1829.		
11 William	"	1831.		
12 Nellie A.	" Feb. 23, 1834.			. . . .
13 Bradford	"	1836.		. . . .
14 Almira	"	1838.		
15 Rebecca	"	1841.		. . . .
16 Daniel	"	1844,	" Feb. 26, 1855.	

4.

SABINA CHAPMAN, born 1815; married James Kelly
of Taunton, Mass.

5.

HIRAM CHAPMAN of Taunton, Mass., born 1817; married Eliza S. Cottrell of Tiverton, R. I., born Sept. 9
1822.

CHILDREN.

17 Mary E.	b. Nov. 15, 1840.	d. .... 1865.
18 Maria S.	" Oct. 10, 1842.	" June 8, 1846.
19 Hiram B.	" Feb. 22, 1836.	
20 Damon F.	" Oct. 29, 1848.	....
21 Emily M.	" July 5, 1851.	
22 Ruth A.	" April 7, 1854.	....
23 Everett W.	" Feb. 22, 1856.	....
24 Herbert L.	" April 11, 1858.	

8.

CATHERINE CHAPMAN, born 1823; married John A. Adams.

9.

ANDREW CHAPMAN of Taunton, Mass., born 1826; married Maria Lincoln.

10.

MARY J. CHAPMAN, born 1829; married Lorenzo Bushee of Taunton.

12.

NELLIE A. CHAPMAN; born Feb. 23, 1834; married, Feb. 23, 1850, Oliver Bushee of Woonsocket, R. I., born Nov. 26, 1829.

CHILDREN.

25 Annie E.   b. May 10, 1852.   ....

26 Ella E.   b. March 24, 1857.
27 Hattie F.   " Dec. 11, 1858.
28 Cora B.   " April 7, 1866.

17.

MARY E. CHAPMAN, born in Taunton, Mass., Nov. 15, 1840, died 1864; married, 1861, to Jared Chace of Pawtucket, R. I., born Nov. 7, 1839.

CHILDREN.

29 Abby J.   b. April 7, 1862.
30 Edith S.   " Aug. 8, 1863.

21.

EMILY M. CHAPMAN, born in Taunton, Mass., July 5, 1851; married, Jan. 11, 1871, Edward Marvel of North Dighton, Mass., born Sept. 24, 1844.

CHILD.

31 Damon N.   b. Dec. 11, 1871.

Descendants of Throop Chapman.

THERE are some grounds for the belief that Ralph Chapman had other children than those given in the record. The writer has never seen the original record, but has been told by a person who has seen it, that it is very much worn by frequent handling, and that "there were other names, but they could not be deciphered." The fact that Ralph mentions in his will the "children John and Samuel," and the probability of there having been no children of those names in the second generation at the time of the making of the will, is strong evidence in favor of the belief.

Noticing an inquiry in the *New England Historical and Genealogical Magazine* in regard to the antecedents of a certain Throop Chapman, it occurred to the writer that there might be some connection between the facts above stated and the fact that Throop,* the Christian name of the Chapman referred to, was the surname of a son-in-law of Ralph Chapman. Upon writing to the person making the inquiry, who is a descendant of Throop Chapman, the writer received the following reply:

"I think that there is little doubt about our family

* Written in the records Throop, Troop or Troup.

" being descended from Ralph Chapman, although one
" link is missing in the chain. As to the age of Throop
" Chapman, one of our family remembers to have seen
" him while he (Throop) was on a visit from Reedsville,
" Vt., to Belchertown, Mass. Throop was said to be
" just ninety-one years old; but whether that was in 1821
" or 1823 my informant cannot remember. * * * *

   " By first wife Throop Chapman had Esther, Susannah,
" William, Ebenezer, *Throop*, died Nov. 23, 1775, and
" *Mary Throop* died Nov. 23, 1775.

   " By second wife Throop Chapman had Jonathan,
" *Throop*, born Aug. 1776, Deborah, Sybil, Isaac, *Mary*,
" Dorcas.

   "Among the baptisms recorded in the books of the
" Congregational church in Belchertown, Mass., May
" 7, 1783, are eight children of Throop Chapman, inclu-
" ding Throop and Mary Throop. The determination
" to perpetuate these two names is certainly remarkable
" if there is no relation between this family and that of
" Ralph Chapman."

Index to the Chapman Family.

Names of Persons who have Married into the Chapman Family.